BRITISH RAILWAY DIESEL MEMORIES

No. 69: D FOR DIESELS:

GAVIN MORRISON

Copyright Book Law Publications 2014

ISBN 978-1-909625-28-0

INTRODUCTION

Unlike our earlier albums of D for Diesels, DD6 is compiled from the photographic archive of just one man – Gavin Morrison. Over the years Gavin has been responsible for putting together dozens of albums which have featured diesel or steam locomotives and which, in the main, have covered specific classes. In this album Gavin has chosen images which cover most of the diesel locomotive classes working on British Railways during the transition period of the 1960s. We have the usual crop of new ex-makers diesels, alongside illustrations of locomotives which have put in some work since their introduction. Nearly every class is covered, from the Drewry 0-6-0DMs to the mighty 'Deltics' with virtually everything else in between. You will not be disappointed because not only are the images of great interest, they are technically superb. Enjoy this latest addition to this on-going series.

David Allen, Newstead, July 2014.

Cover See page 8

Title page **A couple of 'Peaks' D35 and D98, await their next duties at Leeds Holbeck depot on 6th August 1961. Under TOPS D35 became 45117, after having ETH fitted, whilst D98 became 45059 in the seemingly random but actually logical renumbering of the class. D35 was just over a month old when this picture was taken and was soon to be officially allocated to Bath Road depot in Bristol. It survived until May 1986 working finally from Toton depot. D98 entered traffic in April 1961 and was withdrawn in March 1986, also from Toton. Both of the Type 4s ended up in the same scrapyard in Leicester.**

Printed and bound by The Amadeus Press, Cleckheaton, West Yorkshire

First published in the United Kingdom by Book Law Publications, 382 Carlton Hill, Nottingham, NG4 1JA

Drewry shunter D2264 is seen at Hammerton Street depot in Bradford on 8th January 1958. Just over a week old - it was new to the depot on 28th December last – the 0-6-0 diesel-mechanical arrived with sister D2265 from the Robert Stephenson & Hawthorn works at Darlington. Members of the TOPS Class 04, the class first appeared in 1952 from Vulcan Foundry and was in production until 1961. Most examples had a short career with BR and none received TOPS numbers. Many were sold to private industry and no less than eighteen of them are now in preservation! D2264 was withdrawn in October 1969 from Neville Hill depot and cut up at C.F. Booths yard in Rotherham in August 1970. A couple of other things worthy of note in this illustration are the resident steam locomotives which were evicted that very month, and the wrong facing BR crest adorning the cabside of the new diesel!

Staying at 56G on that early January day in 1958, this illustration is a record of the only occasion that English Electric Type 1s were allocated to the diesel multiple unit maintenance depot at Hammerton Street. It is possibly also the only time that any member of the class ever visited the establishment. D8010 (new 19th October 1957) and D8011 (new 2nd November 1957) were both fairly fresh at the time of the Bradford visit and spent about six weeks on loan from Devons Road depot in London; they returned south on 22nd February 1958. The pair were present at 56G to carry out fume tests [believed to be for carbon monoxide] together with Gresley Pacific No.60081 SHOTOVER (why an A3 you might wonder?) in the tunnels on the old Great Northern line between Queensbury and Keighley, which had lost its passenger services in 1954. D8010 [later 20010] survived in traffic until 9th December 1991, with D8011 [20011] lasting until 2nd February 1987. It then passed into Departmental stock but does appear to have been used and was eventually scrapped in early 1994.

The first ten of the 200 English Electric Type 4 main-line diesels were shared between Stratford depot in East London – D200 to D205 – for working the expresses from Liverpool Street to Norwich, and Hornsey depot in North London – D206 to D209 – for East Coast main line workings. D206 was new in 1958 but moved to Stratford in April 1960. Here, on 2nd August 1957, when only a month old, it is seen climbing to Stoke Summit on the ECML past Great Ponton station; the station closed to passengers a month after this picture was taken. D206 was shared between the London Midland and Eastern regions after 1967 and was employed mainly on freight duties. It was withdrawn from Healey Mills depot in March 1983.

D8400 was the first of ten diesel-electric Type 1 Bo-Bos built by the North British Locomotive Co., Glasgow during 1958. They were fitted with 800 h.p. Paxman 16YHXL engines and had a tractive effort of 42000lb, weighing in at 68 tons; the maximum speed was 60 mph. Like most of the other North British diesels they were thoroughly unreliable. D8400 arrived at Doncaster works for acceptance trials on Tuesday 3rd June 1958. During the period of trials it failed on two occasions and was sent back to NBL at Glasgow. It had returned to Doncaster Works by 17th August 1958 where it is shown in the yard in front of the paint shop. After another two attempts on acceptance trials it was eventually put into service; three months after being taken into stock! All the class were allocated to Stratford depot, but they spent much of their time out of use under repair or in store. Being a small non-standard class, the first (D8404) was withdrawn in February 1968 with the rest following by September. All but two were scrapped by G Cohen at Kettering. It will be noted that D8400 is wearing a wrong-facing BR crest which considering it was delivered to BR in June 1958, is a long time after BR was notified by the College of Heralds that the right facing crest was wrong.

This 13th September 1958 picture shows Type 1 Bo-Bo D8200 outside its home depot at Devons Road in East London. This establishment was the first BR purpose-built diesel maintenance depot and became operational in 1958. Coded 1D in the London Midland Region listing under Willesden, the depot only lasted until 1964, which must have made it a candidate for one of the shortest used diesel depots in the country. Once again, the first ten of a class come to the fore and the first ten of this particular class, D8200-D8209, were all allocated to Devons Road, the remainder of the forty-four strong class being initially allocated to the Eastern Region depots at Stratford, King's Lynn, Ipswich, Norwich, and Finsbury Park, although all were eventually concentrated on Stratford depot from where they were withdrawn. British Thomson Houston – BTH – was awarded the contract for the class, with the bodies being constructed at the Yorkshire Engine Co in Sheffield to a specification drawn up by Clayton Equipment Co., Derby. They were classified as Type 1s with 800 h.p. engines, supplied by Paxman – type 16YHXL! With hindsight it appears they were not properly tested and they proved unreliable; tests were carried out on the Settle & Carlisle line. They were designed for trip working and empty stock movements, although they did appear on passenger duties in the summer months. With the type of work for which they were built rapidly disappearing around the London area in the early 1960s, withdrawals were inevitable and the first was taken out of service in March 1968 with the rest following during the next three years. Under TOPS they became Class 15 but none survived long enough to be renumbered. Four members of the class were transferred into Departmental stock for carriage heating duties and moved to numerous depots around the country performing such tasks. One, D8233 has survived into preservation.

Brand new 'Baby Deltic' D5902 is seen in Doncaster Works on 3rd May 1959, prior to delivery to Hornsey depot, and the start of a troublesome career. Perhaps the order in which these Bo-Bos were delivered should have been an omen of what was about to unfold. D5902 arrived at Doncaster on 1st May but had been preceded by D5903 and D5904 on 24th April. D5900 and D5901 did not turn up until 22nd May! D5905, D5906 and D5907 all arriving before the class leaders; only D5908 and D5909 brought a semblance of order back to the dates. The hiccup in delivery all stemmed from English Electric having to cut down the working order weight of the locomotives which were initially a couple of tons over the design weigh. Classified 23 under TOPS, they were a scaled down version of the Co-Co 'Deltics.' They were Bo-Bos fitted with a Napier T9-29 nine-cylinder engine and had a tractive effort of 47000lb. Designed for a maximum speed of 75mph, they were used on services out of King's Cross to Hitchin and Cambridge. Their reliability was so poor that in 1962 they were relegated to trip and shunting duties. As 1963 dawned half the class were in store, and by July all were out of traffic. They were taken back to Vulcan Foundry for refurbishing which took over 12 months. Returned to Finsbury Park depot, they were diagrammed for semi-fast and local stopping services from Kings Cross. The first withdrawal came in 1968 and all were gone by 1972, except D5901 which went into Departmental stock, surviving in that role until 1975. The class can only be considered as a failure and I am sure English Electric wish they had never been built. A group based at Barrow Hill are currently making good progress rebuilding a Class 37 into a Class 23!

Alongside the 'Baby Deltic' at Doncaster on that 3rd May 1959, was Brush Type 2 D5528 which was ready to go to Norwich to start its long 42-year career. The first batch of twenty locomotives entered service between October 1957 and October 1958, all being allocated to Stratford depot. They had the A1A-A1A wheel arrangement, weighed between 107 and 113 tons depending on which batch and were powered by a Mirrlees V-type 12-cylinder engine [JVS12T] rated at 1250 h.p. These gave good service. A decision was taken to up-rate new locomotives to 1365 h.p., which initially appeared successful but in due course started to give a lot of expensive trouble. One locomotive was rated at 2000 h.p., which produced a Type 4 performance! It was decided to replace 200 locomotives with English Electric 1470 h.p. 12SVT engines. These were very successful and the entire class of 263 locomotives were duly altered. Originally intended for the Eastern Region, the Brush Type 2s were eventually used all over the network, but only occasionally in Scotland. Under TOPS they became Class 31 and several of them were fitted with electric train heating [ETH] and were reclassified Class 31/4s; other subclasses followed when modifications were made. D5528 was renumbered 31110 in February 1974 and continued in service until February 2001 receiving the name TRACTION MAGAZINE in September 1999.

These 225 h.p. diesel-hydraulic 0-4-0 shunters were built by the North British Locomotive Company between August 1957 and March 1961 and consisted seventy-three locomotives numbered D2708 to D2780. D2758 is seen on Eastfield depot in Glasgow on 19th June 1960 shortly after delivery. Working for all of its short life from 65A, D2758 was eventually withdrawn in early February 1968 and sold to G.H. Campbell of Airdrie being broken up in November. These were the last locomotives to be built in Scotland for BR. Some of the class left the country for employment at either Crewe locomotive works or the carriage works at Wolverton but none of these faired any better than those still north of the border. At least two of the class have been preserved – in England!

By the middle of 1960 the North Eastern Region had around forty of the English Electric Type 4s allocated and these were based at either York or Gateshead depots. On 26th June 1960, two of the York allocation, D253 and D258, are seen on the shed. D253 was an early withdrawal in August 1976 [as 40053] after being involved in an accident. It was sent to Crewe where it was cut up in November that year. D258, which became 40058, had a much longer career and continued in service until September 1984. Likewise scrapped at Crewe, D258 spent more than three years on the scrap line before it was finally cut-up in 1988.

A seemingly almost new BRC&W Type 2, D5344, is seen outside the repair shop at St Rollox shed [also known as Balornock] on Friday 12th August 1960. Allocated to Inverness at the time when this image was captured on film, the Bo-Bo was simply clean even after nearly ten months in service. New to Haymarket in October 1959, it went to Inverness during the following February but returned to Edinburgh in April for six weeks or so before moving back to 60A. In November 1960 D5344 was transferred to St Rollox (the only member of the class to do so) but went back to Inverness in February 1961. The first twenty of the forty-seven members of the class were allocated to Hornsey depot whilst the remainder went to Haymarket in Edinburgh. Towards the end of 1960 all the class was allocated to Scotland where they continued to work into the 1990s. They are probably best remembered for the work they did on the Highland lines, where they dominated the services for thirty years before the Sprinter multiple units arrived. D5344, as 26044, had a premature end after catching fire between Blair Atholl and Dalwhinnie on Tuesday 17th January 1984. Other members of the class suffered the same fate as did the similar Class 27s.

A portrait of English Electric Type 4 D285 at Darlington shed on 5th March 1961, when it was only eight months old. New to York on the 18th July 1960, D285 spent the majority of its working career allocated to either York or Gateshead depots, a situation which ended on 31st March 1984 when, as 40085, it transferred to Longsight depot in Manchester where it was allocated for its last eleven months of operational life.

The first of the production batch of 'Peaks, D11 and D12 were sent – on paper - to Camden depot for less than a week during October 1960 (in actuality they remained based at Derby) before moving onto Holbeck and Neville Hill depots at Leeds, where they were to be based on and off, along with other class members up to D31, until mid-1973. After crew training had taken place, as shown in this picture of 9th March 1961 when they were both allocated to 55H, they took over the expresses on the Settle & Carlisle line working to Glasgow and Edinburgh, besides those to St Pancras, Birmingham and Bristol. D12 [later No 45011] is seen passing the signal box at Armley Canal to the north of Leeds, hauling train No.N580 which consisted of 12 non-corridor coaches, used for this crew training working during the week, from Leeds to Appleby and return. This train ran for some time to train crews on EE Type 3s and 4s, as well as the 45s. The power station which attracted a lot of coal traffic is just out of the picture to the right. The picture was taken from the flyover in the days when the line had four tracks to Shipley. D11, as 45122, was withdrawn at the end of April 1987. D12 went much earlier in May 1981!

Just one year, and ten days old, 'Peak' D31 waits outside Leeds (City) station on 27th June 1962 ready to take over the Down working of the *THAMES-CLYDE EXPRESS*. Allocated to Neville Hill depot at the time when this photograph was recorded, the Type 4 transferred to Holbeck on 8th December 1962. D31 was the first of the Derby built locomotives to be fitted with the central headcode box, rather than the split box type. The big diesel, renumbered 45030 under TOPS, remained on the Holbeck allocation until May 1973 when it moved to Tinsley, from where it was withdrawn in November 1980.

In the 1960s some of the Newcastle-Liverpool Trans Pennine expresses were routed via Ripon-Harrogate-Wetherby or Horsforth. Here, on 11th April 1961, the 9.45 a.m. from Newcastle is climbing into Harrogate headed by Gateshead EE Type 4 D278. After these services went over to diesel haulage in early 1961, the EE Type 4s were the regular power until mid-1962 when Gateshead depot received an allocation of Brush traction motor equipped 'Peaks' which became Class 46. D278 remained allocated to the North Eastern Region for its entire career which ended on 23rd August 1981: the NER became part of the Eastern Region in 1966.

The famous Heaton to Red Bank empty newspaper van train was especially interesting in steam days for the wide variety of classes and combinations which were used to haul it. The last official steam working was on 3rd July 1966, but prior to this date steam and diesel were seen double heading west of York. Even in diesel days a wide variety of classes were used but not double-headed. The train contained the vans that had been used during the night before to take the newspapers from Manchester to the north east, with the return working usually loading from 20 to 23 vans. Gateshead allocated Type 4 D273 passes through the centre road at York heading south on the train on 5th June 1960. D273 [which became 40073] continued in service until 12th June 1983.

At the north end of York on 26th June 1960, another Gateshead allocated Type 4, D239 is heading a Down King's Cross-Newcastle express past the steam shed yard. The Minster can just be seen to the left of the locomotives' front nose. D239 was an early withdrawal for the class in January 1976, and carried the TOPS number 40039 while still in green livery.

17

It was not until March 1960 that the Scottish Region received its first English Electric Type 4s – D260 to D266 – which were all allocated to Haymarket depot. Another batch of twelve – D357 to D368 – followed between August and December 1961. They were regularly employed on the Edinburgh-Aberdeen expresses as well as a wide variety of other duties. A few, including D266 spent their entire careers working from Haymarket depot, while the others were transferred away to the London Midland Region before withdrawal. D266 is at the head of a Down express van train approaching Drem on Friday 14th July 1961. This view shows the locomotive in its original guise with no route indicators and that useless little ladder which was removed from all of them so fitted in latter years; D260 to D266 were each later fitted with four-character headcode boxes to bring them in line with the Scottish Region batch D358-368 based at Haymarket. The short branch to North Berwick can be seen passing under the bridge. D266 was withdrawn on 5th April 1981 as 40066.

The 'Peaks' took over the Anglo-Scottish expresses north of Leeds at the beginning of the summer timetable in 1961. During the following winter months there were frequent failures of their train heating boilers which resulted in steam substitutions, especially if failures occurred north of the border. D15 is approaching Hellifield with the Down working of *THE THAMES-CLYDE EXPRESS*, complete with headboard, on 29th June 1961 during that inaugural summer. New on 10th December 1960, D15 [which became 45018] was allocated to Holbeck depot from 8th December 1962 and resided there for twelve years before being transferred away. It was finally withdrawn on 4th January 1981 at Tinsley depot.

The Up *FLYING SCOTSMAN* races south past Drem headed by 'Deltic' D9004 when the Co-Co was only two months old. It was allocated to Haymarket shed, 64B, when new and remained until transfer to York depot came in May 1979. D9004 received the name QUEEN'S OWN HIGHLANDER at Inverness station on 23rd May 1964. Renumbered 55004 in May 1974, the big diesel put in twenty-seven months at York before withdrawal took place on 31st August 1981. It was reinstated two days later but failed at Liverpool (Lime Street) on 30th October 1981 and was withdrawn for the second and final time! The line to the right of the locomotive is the start of the North Berwick branch.

Gateshead allocated EE Type 4 D246 leaving Reston station on 15th July 1961 with a Down semi-fast service for Edinburgh, which consisted a wide variety of coaches. Reston station, 12 miles north of Berwick on the ECML, was once the junction for the line to St Boswells but it lost its passenger services on the 4th May 1964. D246 [later 40046] was transferred to the LM Region in January 1967 moving several times therein before withdrawal in February 1983. That event however was not the end of its career, as it was sent on loan to the Ministry of Defence for training exercises at Moreton-on-Lugg, near Hereford, until June 1986. It was eventually broken up in August 1987.

The first regular workings of the 'Deltics' were on the Edinburgh (Waverley)-Newcastle (Central)-London (King's Cross) services. However, during July 1961, D9003 which had been named MELD, without ceremony, at Doncaster Works on the 7th July, appeared at Leeds (Central) with a test train, prior to the class being diagrammed on the *WEST RIDING LIMITED*. It is shown on 18th July 1961 approaching Holbeck (High Level) station site – closed 7th July 1958 – heading the test train on its way back to London. This was probably the first visit of a production 'Deltic' to Leeds. Apart from a few months on loan and allocated to Haymarket, MELD spent its working career firstly at Hornsey and then Finsbury Park, until withdrawn on 30th December 1980; due to a broken fan drive!

'Deltic' D9005 is shown on 2nd August 1961 at its home depot Gateshead when only three months old. It was new on the 25th May 1961, but over two years and four months were to pass before it received the name THE PRINCE OF WALE'S OWN REGIMENT OF YORKSHIRE during a ceremony at York station on 8th October 1963. D9005 [late 5505] remained allocated to Gateshead until May 1973, when many of the class moved to York. It was withdrawn officially on the 3rd February 1982 and cut up at Doncaster by the end of the month. 23

From the early 1960s, the West Coast expresses were starting to be dominated by the English Electric Type 4s and on 5th August 1961, No D325 is at the head of the Up *ROYAL SCOT* which is descending Shap bank and approaching Scout Green. New in December 1960, D325 was the first of the Vulcan Foundry built locomotives to be fitted with the split headcode boxes. Initially allocated to Crewe North, D325 transferred to Camden at the end of January 1961 and remained there (excepting a three-week loan to Upperby in July 1963) until Bescot beckoned on 1st January 1966. Although displaced from the top passenger duties on the West Coast main line by electrification, the class kept a presence on the London Midland Region throughout their lives, most ending their days working freight and parcels traffic. Withdrawn from Springs Branch depot in May 1981, our subject was cut up at Swindon Works in December 1983 as 40125.

The usual group of young 'spotters' are present at the end of Leeds (City) platform on 19th September 1961 as 'Peak' D26 prepares to leave with the Down *THAMES CLYDE EXPRESS*. It was one of the twenty of the class allocated to the Leeds area during 1961 and from where they put in some twelve years service hauling the Anglo-Scottish expresses over the Settle & Carlisle route as well as services to St Pancras and the West Country. According to an ex-fitter who worked at Holbeck in the 1960s, D26 [later 45020] was considered one of the best of the bunch, in spite of suffering two minor fires. It was eventually withdrawn on 11th December 1985.

Leeds Copley Hill steam shed – 56C – can be seen in the background with a class A1 Pacific and a local J50 0-6-0T outside. Behind the A1 can be seen carriages and the carriage sheds, all demolished many years ago and now occupied by industrial premises. On 19th September 1961, 'Deltic' D9003 MELD is passing with three coaches and a van on the 2.05 p.m. local service from Leeds (Central) to Doncaster, which was being used for crew training at the time.

Twenty-six of these English Electric engined 0-6-0 diesel-electric 350 h.p. shunters were built between 1949 and 1952 at Ashford for use on the Southern Region. Having already put in twelve years work at Norwood Junction depot, No.15213 is shown ex-works on Eastleigh shed on 29th September 1961 ready for another seven years service of which most will be performed at hither Green from January 1962. No.15213 was withdrawn on 3rd November 1968. Becoming Class 12 under the TOPS scheme, none of the class were actually renumbered having been condemned entirely by 1971. Note the Bulleid type wheels which would not raise any eyebrows considering which workshop built the class.

The flat countryside to the north of York is featured in this picture of the East Coast Main Line at Beningborough on 17th March 1962. Sulzer Type 2 D5159 is heading south on the Up slow with a long train of empty flat wagons bound for one of the steel plants in south Wales. The Bo-Bo went new to Thornaby depot on 27th June 1961, eventually being transferred to the Scottish Region in January 1972, where it remained until withdrawn in July 1980.

A Bristol-Newcastle express has just left the East Coast Main on 30th March 1962 at Northallerton on the station avoiding line, to take the coastal route to Newcastle via Stockton, Hartlepool and Sunderland; BR Sulzer Type 4 D39 is at the head of the train. Going new to Derby in July 1961, by the date of this picture the 'Peak' was allocated to 82A Bath Road depot in Bristol, along with D33 to D42. They all moved back to the Midland Lines four years later. It was withdrawn in February 1988 after the main generator blew up!

The BRC&W Sulzer Type 2s will forever be associated with the Scottish Region, where they were all eventually allocated. The first twenty of what became Class 26, D5300–D5319, were allocated to the Eastern Region at Hornsey before they were transferred north of the border around 1960. The first twenty-two of what became Class 27, D5347–D5369 went new to Scotland, but the following ten, D5369–D5378, were allocated to Thornaby; the remaining thirty-seven, D5379–D5415 going initially to Cricklewood 14A before dispersing to other Midland Lines depots. All were allocated to Scotland by the end of the 1960s and they remained working virtually every route until withdrawal. One of the Thornaby locomotives, a virtually new D5375, is seen on the Northallerton avoiding line on 30th March 1962, heading an Up freight; the passenger station on the ECML can just be seen in the background. D5375 became 27028 and continued in service until August 1984.

One of the stylish Western Region Hymek diesel-hydraulics is seen at Weymouth shed in the company of a 'Merchant Navy' Pacific on 20th April 1962; the B-B would have worked in on a service from Bristol to the seaside resort. D7018 arrived at Swindon from Beyer, Peacock for acceptance trials on 10th January 1962, to start its somewhat short BR career which ended on 19th March 1975. It was the last of the class to be withdrawn and was sold to the Great Western Society for preservation at Didcot.

D151, one of the fifty-six 1Co-Co1s constructed with Brush traction motors and main generator [they later became Class 46 under TOPS] is approaching Saltaire station non-stop on 13th April 1962 with an Up Morecambe-Leeds train. At this time these trains were usually loaded from six to ten coaches, quite a difference from the 2-car d.m.u.s and Pacers which replaced them. Saltaire station was closed on the 22nd March 1965,but was re-opened nineteen years later on 9th April 1984 having been rebuilt. D151 [later 46014] was allocated to the London Midland, Western and then Eastern regions, before being withdrawn from Gateshead depot on 3rd May 1984.

From the road bridge just to the south of Doncaster station a fine view is obtained of the 'Plant' works offices and the station area. Unnamed 'Deltic' D9019 is departing with an Up Leeds (Central)-London (Kings Cross) express on Sunday 29th April 1962. This particular 'Deltic' put in twelve and a half years allocated to Haymarket depot before withdrawal from York depot on 31st December 1981.It was named ROYAL HIGHLAND FUSILIER at Glasgow (Central) station on 11th September 1965. Fortunately it is preserved by the Deltic Preservation Society – DPS – and has performed on the Network many times. Also of interest in the picture is a BTH Type 1 Bo-Bo awaiting a visit to the works and in the distance, a 350 h.p. 0-6-0DE shunter is hauling a newly built West Coast electric locomotive, probably a class AL5 Bo-Bo [later Class 85], towards the departure sidings. Steam is represented by a solitary Peppercorn A1, one of Doncaster's own, No.60157 GREAT EASTERN which was main line pilot for the day – a 36A duty – just a week after coming off works.

Photographed whilst I was on a regular Sunday visit to Doncaster shed and works, this brand new English Electric Type 3, D6736, was in the works yard awaiting entry into service at Hull Dairycoates depot on 29th April 1962. The Co-Co was renumbered 37036 in March 1974 before being modified to the sub-class 37/5 as 37507 and named HARTLEPOOL PIPE MILL in 1987. It was eventually sold to Direct Rail Services in April 2002 becoming one of their class 37/6s, as 37605. So, as of to-day 10th October 2013, some fifty-one years after this picture was taken, it is still in regular use on the network. I think that says an awful lot about the quality of the build of English Electric locomotives.

On 1st May 1962, one of Holbeck's batch of twenty 'Peaks' D15 is shown passing the site of Holbeck (Low level) station ,which closed on 7th July 1958, and which was not that far from the centre of Leeds. In the background can be seen the bridge carrying the former Great Northern line into Leeds (Central) station, which closed on the 29th April 1967.The driver has just opened up the locomotive producing an exhaust as it heads for Carlisle and Edinburgh via the Waverley route. D15 arrived at Leeds in late February 1961, firstly allocated to Neville Hill but moving across the city to Holbeck in December 1962 where it remained for over seventeen years. Renumbered 45018 in July 1974, it was eventually withdrawn on the 4th January 1981 at Tinsley depot.

On a glorious early summer day in Oban, 12th May 1962, BRC&W Type 2 D5352 is receiving little attention from the gathered enthusiasts' that have travelled from Glasgow on a special hauled by two of the preserved Scottish steam locomotives, namely the famous Caledonian Single 4-2-2 No.123 and ex-North British No.256 GLEN DOUGLAS both of which can be seen to the left of the picture. D5352 was heading an afternoon service to Glasgow (Buchanan Street), via the Callander and Oban route, over Glen Ogle. One of the early batch of Type 2s, it was allocated to Scotland from new, arriving in September 1961. It became 27006 in the TOPS scheme and spent its entire career allocated to Glasgow's Eastfield depot. It had something of an inglorious end when it caught fire [not entirely unknown for the BRC&W Type 2s] and was scrapped in January 1977.

I have already commented on the size of the Morecambe-Leeds services at this period on page 32, but here, on 4th June 1962, we see an exceptional example of twelve coaches – the train is an early afternoon departure from Morecambe to Leeds – quite a contrast as already mentioned to the current usual two or three-car 'Pacer'. The location is just north of Keighley where the local golf course is situated. BR Sulzer Type 4 D162 was less than two months old at the time and was allocated to Derby. After 1968 D162 was re-allocated to the Western Region where it remained until withdrawal came, for the first time, on 14th December 1980. It was re-instated in November 1981 and then withdrawn again on 29th April 1982. Most unusually it was re-instated yet again for a third time less than a month later in May 1982, operating from Gateshead depot. Renumbered 46025 in February 1974, the big diesel was finally condemned on 25th November 1984.

Some of our regular readers might note a similarity between this illustration and the image which appeared on page 37 of *'D' For Diesels:4*. This image is dated 16th June 1962 whereas the other is alas undated. However, the train 1E81 is the same train and the motive power combination is the same but with different locomotives. The immaculate Brush Type 2 in this photograph is D5657 of Darnall depot and just like the earlier image it is in sharp contrast to the rather dirty Thompson B1 4-6-0 No.61145 of Doncaster shed, as they provide more than sufficient power for the seven-coach train leaving York for Sheffield. The location is the old racecourse station, last used for race going passengers on the 24th August 1939. Once the summer timetable was completed D5657 transferred to Stratford on 23rd September 1962 and that was the last Sheffield saw of it for some years. Renumbered 31230 in March 1974, the Brush continued working regularly until 1991 when it began a series of periods in storage. It was removed from the rolling stock records on 17th March 2000. Now, has anyone come up with a reasonable explanation of that front bracket yet?

The caption on page 30 mentioned that nine of the BRC&W Type 2s, D5370 – D5378 were delivered new to Thornaby depot between 17th January and 7th March 1962. Eventually, in January 1966, they all went to the East Midlands, swapped for a similar number of consecutively numbered Sulzer Type 2s. Here at York on 16th June 1962, D5371 and D5374 are coming off the avoiding line at the south end of the station with an Up steel train from Teesside, which they would work as far as Dringhouses yard. Moving to Scotland before the decade was out, D5371 became 27005 and was withdrawn in June 1987; D5374 actually received two numbers – 27101 in April 1974, and 27045 in September 1984 – before withdrawal due to accident damage in May 1986.

The first twenty-five Sulzer Type 2s which became TOPS Class 25, D5151 to D5175, were fitted with 1250 h.p. Sulzer 6LDA28B engines and AEI 137BX traction motors and associated equipment. Built at Darlington, they were all allocated to Thornaby depot from new between April 1961 and April 1962, before being spread all over the network. D5170 [later 25020] is hauling a very lengthy van train on the Up slow of the East Coast Main Line at Beningborough on 16th June 1962. D5170 was allocated to the NE and Eastern Region for the whole of its working career and was withdrawn in January 1976.

This picture, also recorded on 16th June 1962, is taken from the same spot as the previous image, but looking south. 'Deltic' D9007 PINZA, new on 22nd June 1961, will have reached 100 m.p.h. after York on the Down *HEART OF MIDLOTHIAN*. This was then the main late afternoon express from London (King's Cross) to Edinburgh (Waverley). D9007 was one of the Finsbury Park racehorses, as their allocation became known, as all were named after racehorses continuing the LNER tradition. Renumbered 55007 in February 1974, the 'Deltic' moved to York in May 1981 but only put in a further seven months service before being withdrawn on the final day of the year.

Eastfield based EE Type 1 D8114 was allocated to the Glasgow depot when new in February 1962, and here on the following 14th July it has just passed the Beattock summit sign of 1015 feet with an Up Saturday evening fitted freight. It was a Scottish Region locomotive for the majority of its career but was finally allocated to Toton where it ended its career in January 1990.

The summer of 1962 was really the last one where the English Electric Type 4s were diagrammed to work many of the East Coast Main Line passenger services, together with the 'Deltics' which were all in service by then. The Brush Type 4s which became Class 47s, and to a lesser degree the BR Sulzer Type 4s which were later classified Class 46 under TOPS, rapidly took over many of the workings from 1963. D241, allocated to Gateshead when new in October 1959, has just emerged from Stoke tunnel with an Up express on 21st July 1962.

By the middle of 1960 the ten Pilot Scheme 'Peaks' which had been working some West Coast Main Line passenger services had all been moved to Toton, leaving the English Electric Type 4s to work the diesel diagrams, including some Trans-Pennine duties. D214, which entered service in June 1959, and received the name ANTONIA in May 1961, is shown passing through the Lune Gorge on 18th August 1962, gaining as much speed as possible to tackle Shap bank. It was a LM Region locomotive for its entire career which ended in November 1991.

A clean Haymarket 'Deltic' D9016 eases the Down *QUEEN OF SCOTS PULLMAN* out of Leeds (Central) on 2nd October 1962. The destination was Glasgow (Queen Street), the train travelling via Harrogate and the now closed section of line to Ripon. The train was introduced on the 1st May 1928,but withdrawn during the war; reinstated on the 5th July 1948 it ran until the 13th June 1964. D9016 ran nameless until July 1964, when it received the name GORDON HIGHLANDER, having entered service on the 27th October 1961. It was withdrawn on the 30th December 1981 and passed into preservation, eventually being taken over by Porterbrook , who painted it in a very flamboyant purple livery. Some twenty-one years [2002] after being withdrawn it returned to the main lines on specials.

The only Type 1 centre-cab diesel-electric locomotives to operate on BR were built at Clayton Equipment Co., at Hatton near Tutbury, in Derbyshire, and International Combustion [Holdings] Ltd., Derby. Numbered D8500 to D8616, they were designated Class 17 under TOPS, but none of them received the 17XXX numbers. All were built between 1962 and 1964, the last batch by Beyer, Peacock in Manchester. Unfortunately for the Scottish Region they were allocated eighty-eight of them from new, the rest going initially to the North Eastern Region and the Eastern Region. Whilst they looked quite attractive, they were, mechanically, a disaster! Most were withdrawn with less than ten years service under their belts, and in many cases they were either in store or under repair. D8502 is shown at Holbeck shed, Leeds on 5th October 1962 whilst on delivery from Derby to Polmadie in Glasgow.

One of the ninety-eight BRC&W Type 3s [later Class 33] D6572 is stabled on Feltham shed on 14th October 1962 when it was exactly one year old. All of the class were allocated to the Southern Region from new and except for a small batch of Sulzer Type 2s allocated during the early years of dieselisation on the SR, the region managed with this single class for all there diesel locomotive requirements. Being so intensely used (although it has been suggested they were under utilised) within SR territory, there were few workings that took them out of the region, where they were very well maintained. This situation changed towards the end of their careers when they appeared along the North Wales coast line, at Manchester (Piccadilly) and on the Portsmouth-Bristol-Cardiff services and the west of South Wales. Renumbered 33054, the Bo-Bo became one of the members of the class to be withdrawn due to accident damage in February 1986.

It is extremely likely that Brush Type 4 D1505 was the first of the class to visit Leeds. It was new in January 1963, arriving at Finsbury Park depot on the 18th, but almost immediately moved to Neville Hill depot at Leeds, for fitter and driver training. Here it is at 55H on 24th March 1963 where it remained until April when it was returned to Finsbury Park. It was allocated to the main ECML depots for most of its career. D1505 became the second member of the class to receive Inter City livery when it received the name RAIL RIDERS in December 1981 as 47406. Withdrawal came in August 1990, but it was not broken up until November 1995.

In their original form the North British built Type 2 diesel-electric Bo-Bos were fitted with NBL/MAN L12V18/21 engines producing 1000 to 1100 h.p. A decision was taken to re-engine some of them after trials with D6123 proved successful. Twenty-nine of them (it was pure coincidence that they became TOPS Class 29 – wasn't it?) received Paxman 12YJXL engines which produced 1350 h.p. They were then put to work on West Highland and Oban line duties as well as on the Glasgow/Dundee/Aberdeen services, and, according to some reports, performed reasonably well. All were withdrawn by October 1971 and they must be regarded as another of the early diesel class disasters, which contributed in no small way to the demise of the famous North British Locomotive Co. A Dundee-Glasgow (Buchanan Street) express is shown approaching Gleneagles station on 11th May 1963, headed by D6122 and D6108. D6122 was officially withdrawn in December 1967, after just over eight years, although it had been out of service for sometime beforehand. D6108 was converted to a Class 29 and was one of the eight to receive BR blue livery. Eighteen months after the new engine was fitted it was in store at Inverurie works scrapyard and withdrawn in May 1969!

This was definitely a day those in charge of the West Highland line in 1963 would want to forget. A special was run from Glasgow to Mallaig, and return; it was definitely going to be the very *last* steam train to work the West Highland Line. It was deemed appropriate that ex-North British locomotives should work the train – big mistake! The only suitable classes available were the preserved GLEN DOUGLAS and some J37 0-6-0s, none of which had done any sustained long distance passenger work, or indeed freight duties for that matter, for some time. Three engines were selected for the job and were given special preparation. The result was: the first failed at Rannoch after running hot; GLEN DOUGLAS continued alone but dropped its firebars, I believe somewhere near Tulloch, which produced the very rare sight of a NBL Type 2 actually rescuing a train rather than the other way round. The special continued to Mallaig with two J37s, one of which was declared a failure upon arrival, meaning three out of the four steam locomotives failed in half a trip, which must be a record! A BRC&W Type 2, D5351 was found to haul the special back to Glasgow, where the passengers arrived, I believe after midnight. The *JACOBITE*, as the special was named, is seen at Mallaig ready for the return journey on 1st June 1963. D5351 became 27005 and was new to Eastfield depot in August 1961. It spent its working career in Scotland and was withdrawn in July 1987, fortunately passing into preservation with the Scottish RPS. Now then, note the intending passengers walking about permanent way!

Carlisle Upperby allocated EE Type 4 D291 manages to pass Shap summit in a brief patch of sunlight on 24th August 1963 as it heads north with a Euston-Carlisle express. It was new to Crewe in August 1960, the 1-Co-Co-1 became 40091 in February 1974 (that was a busy month for the painters) and remained on the LM Region until withdrawn in September 1984.

(above) **Metro-Vick Co-Bo D5714 departs from Preston for the north with a train for the north (destination and date unknown). Possibly the worst of the Pilot Scheme designs, the noisy, unreliable, dirty, overweight Co-Bos were nothing more than a liability. Amazingly one is actually preserved!** *(below)* **In total contrast, the locomotive featured below represents one of the most reliable diesel locomotives ever to run on BR. English Electric Type 3 D6730, allocated to Hull Dairycoates, is shown near Kirkham, on a Saturdays Only Sheffield-Blackpool train on 21st September 1963 – an Illuminations special. At this time it was one of the very few EE Type 3 workings to pass through West Yorkshire. Under the TOPS scheme, D6730 became 37030; later converted to Class 37/7 and renumbered 37701 in December 1986, it was withdrawn in September 2007, aged forty-six!**

Displaying different body styles, two BR Sulzer Type 2s, which became Class 25s, are seen at Leeds Holbeck depot on 10th May 1964. Both diesels were Derby built, D5233, new in December 1963, became 25083 and is seen with D5209 [25059], which entered service 6 months earlier. It is now preserved on the Keighley & Worth Valley Railway. No D5233 also entered preservation at the Caledonian Railway Preservation Society, fifteen years after being withdrawn.

It was mentioned earlier that the SR Type 3 diesels generally did not work far away from the Region. However, the daily Northcliffe–Uddingston cement train was definitely the exception to the rule, as the class worked the loaded train as far as York and the return empties back to Kent at this period. On 29th May 1964 D6528, with York Minster visible just above the train, is passing the steam shed on its way to Clifton yard, where different motive power (usually an EE Type 4) will take over. D6528 was new in October 1960 and after conversion for push-and-pull working, became 33111 in March 1974 under TOPS. Withdrawal came in June 1991 with the locomotive eventually passing into preservation.

Here on 21st September 1963, we see Co-Bo D5708 on a secondary passenger duty working the Lakeside branch and ready to depart for Plumpton Junction and Ulverston. D5708 was new in December 1958, but was withdrawn by September 1968. This station is now part of the Lakeside & Haverthwaite Railway.

Not one of the high profile specials normally associated the West Riding Branch of the Railway Correspondence & Travel Society, but a very leisurely day out on the Derwent Valley Light Railway on 9th January 1965. The railway had run specials over the years for enthusiasts and this one [in fact it was duplicated the following week due to demand] was to mark the closure of the Cliff Common to Wheldrake section, about seven miles of the total length of sixteen. The light railway opened on 19th July 1913 which was the start of a long and interesting tale, which lasted until November 1979. Today a small section has been re-opened as a heritage operation. The 1965 special is seen at Layerthorpe station headed by 0-6-0DM D2111, a shunter which was to become a member of Class 03. Built by BR Doncaster in November 1960, D2111 was hired out to the line. The DM became 03111 November 1973 and continued in service until July 1980 working from Gateshead depot.

As this picture will testify, Sunday or full week-end diversions over the Settle & Carlisle line, when the route over Shap was closed, have been going on for a long time. Headed by English Electric Type 4 D330, the Up *ROYAL SCOT* on 4th April 1965 is seen passing the summit board at Ais Gill showing 1169 feet. One of the twenty built at Vulcan Foundry in 1961 that were fitted with split headcode boxes, D330 eventually became 40130 and spent all of its life on the LM Region before being withdrawn in March 1982.

Metro-Vick Co-Bos were strangers on Holbeck shed and the reason for the presence of this example on 9th June 1965 is unknown. D5705 was new in December 1958, and according to records, spent much time in store during its career, even after rectification. It was officially withdrawn in September 1968 and was sent to Derby RTC becoming S15705. After conversion to an un-powered carriage heating unit, it became TDB 968006 and was withdrawn in September 1977. It then passed into preservation and the long road back to working order.

A nice array of signals and the wide approach to the station at Bournemouth (West), gave a fine location to photograph departures. The station opened in June 1874, but at the date of this picture on 29th August 1965, there was only another five weeks to go before closure. Such famous trains as the *PINES EXPRESS* and *BOURNEMOUTH BELLE* began and finished their journeys here. An Up express for Waterloo is shown ready to leave with BRC&W Type 3 D6565, [later renumbered 33047] which had entered service in August 1961. Like some other members of the class, it was withdrawn in February 1993 due to accident damage. If you stood in the same position today from where this picture was taken, you would be in a highly precarious position on a dual carriageway.

In the days when railway embankments were kept clear of undergrowth and trees, the line between Bournemouth (Central) and Poole was typical of what was to be expected. On 31st August 1965, a Type 3 Hymek is heading a Down inter-regional express and is approaching Gas Works Junction at Branksome. The locomotive is D7015 which had entered service at Bath Road depot in December 1961. The B-B was withdrawn in June 1972, apparently due to accident damage, although no record seems to exist of an accident involving the locomotive having taken place.

By 1965 the two classes of diesel-hydraulic B-B 'Warships' were rapidly being ousted from main line duties on the Western Region, being replaced by diesel-electric Type 4s from Brush and BR Sulzer designs. The Maybach engined 'Warships' found further employment on the Exeter-Waterloo services over the Southern Region displacing steam as the Western Region tried their best to rid itself of the old order west of Salisbury. On 5th March 1966 D818 GLORY, painted now in maroon livery, is seen arriving at Templecombe with an Up express for Waterloo. In an attempt to speed up their prestigious express passenger workings in the late Sixties', the WR once again called upon the 'Warships' to power their expresses but this time working in multiple between London and Plymouth. However, that particular operation was fraught with problems because not all of the B-Bs had compatible multiple unit control gear. Under the TOPS scheme Class numbers 42 and 43 were allocated to the two types of B-B 'Warships' but none of them were ever renumbered in the series. Seventy-one were built between June 1958 and June 1962, they had all been withdrawn before the end of 1972, most during a major cull in 1971. D818 was condemned at the end of October 1972 and afterwards cut up at Swindon.

This is the not so well known Clapham Junction, where the lines from Low Gill on the WCML and Wennington, near Lancaster and Carnforth used to join up. The Low Gill line from Clapham was occasionally used as a diversionary route when engineering work was taking place on the WCML, but it was closed on 18th June 1966. Clapham station is still open. Back in the days of locomotive hauled services between Morecambe/Carnforth and Leeds, Sulzer Type 2 No D7592 is shown calling with an Up afternoon service on 12th March 1966. No D7592 entered service in May 1964 at Toton and was allocated to the LM Region for the whole of its career, which ended in May 1984 at Crewe. Under TOPS it became 25242.

This picture was taken at Holes Bay junction, just to the west of Poole station on 27th July 1966. At the time it was still the point where Somerset & Dorset trains joined the Weymouth-Waterloo main line. Poole harbour is just to the left of this picture and this local freight will have come from Hamworthy goods yard on the other side of the water. Drewry Car Co. 0-6-0DM D2288, which was hauling the train, was built by Robert Stephenson & Hawthorn at Darlington in April 1960 and was initially allocated to Eastleigh depot. In July 1966 it was on the strength of Bournemouth shed and had been for four years or so but was about to transfer back to Eastleigh for a short period. It remained in service until December 1967 when it was condemned at Bournemouth.

D4100, one of twenty-six English Electric powered diesel-electric 0-6-0 shunters which were re-geared from 1959 onwards, and later classified as 09s. They were identical in every way to the ubiquitous Class 08, but were capable of higher speeds (27.5 m.p.h. against 20 m.p.h.). The date is 25th September 1966 and D4100 has just received a major overhaul at Eastleigh works and has been released in BR blue livery with the double-arrow motif replacing the BR crest. Most of the class were initially allocated to the Southern Region but a couple of them resided on the LMR. Under TOPS D4100 became 09012 and it received the name DICK HARDY at an open day at Stewarts Lane depot in April 1988. Un-named in 1990, it was renamed at Selhurst Depot in 1991.

On 28th July 1968, an Up West Coast express has been diverted over the Settle & Carlisle line and is headed by Brush Type 4s D1964 and D1852. The location is half-way between Settle Junction and Long Preston. D1964 was new in September 1965 and was allocated to Newport. It carried fleet numbers 47264, 47619 and 47829 during its career. While it was working for Virgin trains during its latter years, it was painted in a unique white livery for the class, with 'Police' painted on the body sides. It was withdrawn in March 2006, but has only recently been scrapped. D1852 was one of the batch of twenty-five which went new to Crewe in 1965 – D1837- D1861 – and became 47202 under TOPS. The Co-Co came to a premature end after it had been in a collision with Class 33 33032 at Westbury in March 1987.

English Electric Type 4 D336 is shown passing through Dent cutting, just to the north of the station, on 15th February 1969. A pick-up freight headed by Type 4 D415 can just be seen approaching the station. This location is usually one of the first places where the S&C gets blocked during severe snowfalls, as happened 1963. D336, one of the batch fitted with split box head codes from new and entered service in March 1961. It was withdrawn in May 1982.

The fifty English Electric 2700 h.p. Co-Cos built at Vulcan Foundry, Newton-le-Willows during 1967 and 1968 were initially on hire to BR but and later purchased. They were numbered D400 to D449 [later becoming 50001-50050]. The class was based at Crewe for working the West Coast main line services to the north, prior to the introduction of electric traction. They often worked in pairs in order to improve schedules but also because they were not as reliable as had been hoped. D405 – later 50005 and named COLLINGWOOD in April 1978 – approaches Shap summit on 7th March 1970 with the Down *ROYAL SCOT*. The whole class were transferred to the Western Region in 1973 to replace the 'Westerns'. D405, as 50005, continued in service until December 1990.

14th March 1970 was a memorable day on the Woodhead route as five 'Footex' specials were booked over it, because Manchester United were playing an important cup tie at Sheffield Hillsborough. This resulted in an interesting selection of locomotives hauling the specials.. They included two type 2s, D7595 and D7597 as illustrated, two EE Type 4s, D232 and D229, 'Peak' D36 (sans the prefix) and the big surprise being Class 50 D414. In addition during the morning a class 47 passed on a freightliner as well as several Class 76 EM1 electrics. D7595 and D7597 [later 25245 and 25247] are shown just past the level crossing at Torside, with one of the valley reservoirs in the background. They were withdrawn in 1985 and 1983 respectively. It is likely this was the only occasion that a Class 50 travelled over the route. Sadly 'Footex' specials are rare these days, resulting as far as I am concerned, in a complete lack of interest in the game.

The sea wall between Dawlish and Teignmouth is probably one of the most photographed sections of track in the country. 'Warship' D814 DRAGON is shown approaching Teignmouth on a Down empty stock working on 29th August 1972, It entered service in January 1960 at the start of a very short career which only lasted until January1972. However, it was reinstated in May and then withdrawn again in November. Here we see it during its second 'life.'

The tide is out at Dawlish as D1019 WESTERN CHALLENGR heads along the seafront on 1st September 1972 with a Down freight. The locomotive is looking exceptionally clean for a member of this class, because many had very shabby paintwork during their latter years. D1019 was only in service for ten years between May 1963 and May 1973. Seventy-four of these handsome machines were built, all having very short careers because being diesel-hydraulics, they were considered non-standard by BR.

Another view of the Devon foreshore, this time showing D1057 WESTERN CHIEFTAIN approaching Teignmouth with a Down express on 22nd August 1973. D1057 managed thirteen years of service for BR between April 1963 and May 1976; its withdrawal was due to it requiring a new power unit.

Strictly speaking this picture is outside the scope of the book, but the locomotive is still in BR service and running with a 'D' number. D200, the first of the English Electric Type 4s, entered service in March 1958 and started work on the Liverpool Street- Norwich expresses. It remained on the Eastern Region until August 1967 when it was transferred to the LMR. It was withdrawn in August 1981, and was stored at various locations until it was sent to Toton for overhaul in May 1983; it was afterwards re-instated. It then ran many railtours, painted in the BR green livery, but was also regularly used on the 10.40 a.m. Carlisle-Leeds passenger service over the Settle-Carlisle line, returning in the afternoon. Here, on 10th August 1983, it is seen on this working heading south at Keld. Eventually it was withdrawn in April 1988 and presented to the NRM. Since then it has visited many of the heritage railways.